A Rose in Heaven

Dawn Siegrist Waltman

A Rose in Heaven

Dawn Siegrist Waltman

ISBN 1-929678-03-7

Published by Paradise Publications, Paradise, PA
Printed in the United States of America

Dedication

I dedicate this book to the Lord Jesus Christ. Without Him as my personal Lord and Savior there would be no message of hope or healing to share.

A Rose in Heaven is merely a reflection of the work He has done in my life. For this reason, I must acknowledge Him as the true author of this book. With open hands and an open heart, I lay this book before Jesus Christ and ask Him to use it to touch the lives of hurting women. May He, and only He, receive all of the honor and glory.

Dawn Waltman, 1999

I am both humbled and thrilled to see what God has done with *A Rose in Heaven* in just one year. My fervent prayer is that this message of hope and healing would continue to grow and spread – touching the hearts of grieving mothers everywhere.

Dawn Waltman
Second printing, 2001

——— *In Memory* ———————————————

Molly Dawn Waltman
March 25, 1996

Although you never saw the sunshine outside
of your mommy's womb, your little life
touched the lives of so many ... bringing hope,
healing and the promise of heaven.

I love you little Molly,
and I will never forget you.

And in memory of my two precious
babies, Mitchell and Madison, my
tiny rosebuds, carried to heaven
just weeks after your little
lives had begun.

Oh, how I long for the day
when I will see you in full bloom.
Please know that I love you forever.

Molly's precious
footprints.

All my love,
Mommy

Special Thanks

Asa Jolan Beitzel ... Your brief life and death, little Asa, gave me the vision and the courage to finish this book. And for that I am truly thankful. *Linda Stockin* ... For the countless hours you have spent editing this book. Your expertise, insight, advice, counsel, prayers, and friendship have been priceless to me. *Darla Joy Anastasi* ... What can I say to sum up all you have meant to me? Thank you for believing in my dreams and helping to make them come true. *Jim Gochnauer* ... For taking my vision and pulling it all together with thoroughness, professionalism, and true sense of purpose. And finally to *Brian* ... The love of my life and the awesome daddy of our children, both on earth and in heaven. God gave me the best when He gave me you! I love you!

Table of Contents

Letter to a Grieving Mother

Dear friend,

Although you may not know it, I, along with many others, have been praying for you for a long time. Years before this book was in print, I prayed for each hurting mother that would someday hold these meditations in her hands. Women's groups, home groups, and countless individuals have prayed and are praying as you move through this journey of grief. I tell you this so that you will know that angels have been sent out on your behalf. They are surrounding you right now, protecting you, and ministering to you. God loves you so much. He hurts with you and wants to carry you in His arms.

I wrote **A Rose in Heaven** because God placed in my heart a desire to meet a need in the lives of women who are grieving the loss of their baby through miscarriage, stillbirth, or early infant death. Eight years ago I lost two babies to miscarriages. It was such a painful and confusing time in my life. Five years later my little girl was stillborn at twenty weeks. As a result of these losses, God gave me the vision to create a book that would actually serve as a companion for grieving mothers. **A Rose in Heaven** is that vision. These meditations are based on my journey of grief, hope, and healing after the stillbirth of my little girl, Molly. They reflect the many hills, valleys, and plateaus that I encountered during that first and most difficult year. In addition to my writings, five mothers who have also suffered the loss of a baby have contributed meditations entitled "Reflections." Here, these women reflect on a particular element of their own journey and the goodness of God that carried them through. The sole purpose of this resource is to reassure mothers, like yourself, that they are not alone in their feelings of sorrow, anger, and confusion, as well as hope, joy, and healing.

It is unlikely that you will identify with every meditation, but my prayer is that you would be able to identify with many of them. Therefore, you can be comforted with the knowledge that, though your world may seem bleak now, you will feel the sun again as you begin to heal.

God's Word is so awesome. For this reason, each meditation contains a verse that has the power to reach the very core of your being where that healing will begin.

The days and weeks that initially surround the death of your baby will no doubt be filled with prayers of faithful people. It is in the months that follow that a woman often struggles and feels so alone. Although each meditation is based on my heartache three years ago, the prayer at the bottom of each entry is a prayer that I am praying for you now. Please know I am committed to interceding and praying on your behalf.

The meditations are not dated, so turn to them whenever you need to feel the companionship, understanding, and hope of someone who has traveled this difficult journey. Some readings do focus on a specific event, occasion, or struggle that may be particularly difficult that first year. Review the titles so that when a particular event in your life seems exceptionally difficult, you can turn to a meditation that will minister to your heart.

*The title of this book **A Rose in Heaven** is symbolic of the hope that Jesus Christ desires for every hurting mother. Our precious babies are very similar to a tiny rosebud. Perfectly formed, they need only time and nourishment to be born or to bloom. A miscarriage, stillbirth, or early infant death halts that process, and we as mothers never have the blessing of seeing our baby bloom. Although this grief is something you feel like you might never overcome, you must hold on to hope. The hope of Jesus and the hope of seeing your baby healthy, happy, and in full bloom!*

A true Rose in Heaven!

In Jesus' love,
Dawn

The Cords of Death

*The cords of death entangled me, the anguish of
the grave came upon me; I was overcome by
trouble and sorrow* Psalm 116:3

My eyes searched the screen, desperately looking for the pulse of my baby's heartbeat. Only six weeks earlier I had watched with fascination as sonogram waves showed the baby inside my womb, rolling, kicking, and stretching. Now, that same figure was still. A lump formed in my throat as I choked out the words, "My baby's not moving. My baby is dead, isn't it?" I watched the doctor's eyes as he concentrated on the screen while sweeping the silver ball over my swollen womb.

The doctor knew the answer. My husband knew the answer. And I knew the answer before I had even asked the question. My husband gripped my hand as thoughts and emotions swept over me. "Oh God, no! Please, no!" I cried. My body shook with un-controllable sobs as the reality of the motionless figure on the screen sunk in. My baby, my precious baby was dead.

Dear friend,

I am so sorry your baby has died. I wish so desperately I could change what has happened. I have felt your pain so please know I care and I am praying for you. Right now, let God carry you. He won't let go of you. I promise.

Goodbye Kiss

My heart is in anguish within me; the terrors of death
assail me. Oh that I had the wings of a dove!
I would fly away and be at rest. Psalm 55:4,6

As the nurse entered my hospital room with the wheel chair, we knew it was time to say goodbye to our little girl. I had been so strong throughout the evening but now my emotions buckled and collapsed. The reality of leaving Molly and never seeing her again on earth was the most heart wrenching feeling I have ever experienced.

My husband and I wrapped her blanket snugly around her tiny body, trying to remember every detail of her little face. After several minutes, I finally kissed her forehead and laid her on the bed. She looked so tiny and vulnerable lying by herself on that big bed. I kept my eyes on the little bundle as the nurse pushed my wheelchair out of the room, trying desperately to keep her in my sight as long as I could. In a couple seconds, though, we were out the door and my little girl was gone.

When I left Molly in that room, I left part of my heart with her. At that very moment, I knew I would never be the same again.

Dear friend,
It's okay to feel like running away. It hurts so much to lose your child. But as you run, run into the arms of Jesus. Cling to Him. He wants to hold you close.

4

Resurrection Power

*For the Lord Himself will come down from heaven, with
a loud command, with the voice of the archangel and
with the trumpet call of God, and the dead in
Christ will rise first.* 1 Thessalonians 4:16

The sun was bright and the air crisp and cool as we gathered around the grave site. Our pastor laid his hand on the tiny white casket and then spoke these words with boldness and assurance:

"For as much as the spirit has departed this body, we do commit all that is mortal of our sister to its resting place in the earth. But the spirit of our sister which is the true person, we commit to God who alone knows the secrets of the resurrection and life eternal. Knowing that at the second coming of Jesus, the dead in Christ shall rise first and we who are alive and remain will be caught up with them in the clouds to meet the Lord in the air."

I was totally caught off guard at the thought of our baby breaking out of the grave with a new body. Sure, I believed in the resurrection of God's people, but I had never given thought to how that promise applied to Molly. An awesome feeling of God's power washed over me as I took a moment and allowed my mind to entertain that very thought. The new body of our Molly, breaking out of the very spot where we were standing! What an incredible promise!

Dear friend,

It's true! Because of God's power you and I will both see our babies again. Hallelujah! I pray with all my heart that you would know and take joy in that promise today!

Reckless Words

Reckless words pierce like a sword. Proverbs 12:18

"Well, look at it this way, there was probably something wrong with the baby anyway."

"You are still young, you can have more children."

I had been warned that I would probably hear comments like these, but somehow when I heard them with my own ears, I felt as if they had pierced my heart. I stared at the person speaking to me and thought to myself, " You have no idea what you are talking about!"

It doesn't matter if my baby had a birth defect or not! She was my child! And I was her mother! Do people think I would love her less if she was not *perfect*?

I know I am young and can possibly have more children, but what does that have to do with the death of this child? Sometimes I want to say, "Don't you get it? This was not an appliance that didn't work that I will return for a replacement. This was a baby – my baby. And now my baby is dead."

Dear friend,

I pray that our Lord Jesus would protect your heart by allowing all reckless words to fall only on deaf ears.

Freedom to Grieve

*And let us consider one another in order to stir up
love and good works.* Hebrews 10:24

I lay across the bed sobbing at the rawness of my pain. It hurt
so much. Mingled in with the grief was a stab of bitterness as I
listened to the buzz of my husband's power tools. Three days
earlier our baby had died. Three days! So why was he "up and
at 'em" as if nothing happened? Where were the signs of his pain
and his grief? Didn't he understand what we had lost? Or was he
so preoccupied with the construction project that he had already
forgotten about our baby? The addition itself was even a source
of pain. We had started the project because our family was ex-
panding and we needed more room. So much for expanding!

Suddenly, I realized the tools were silent. I heard the floor
creak and looked up to see Brian coming into the room. Walking
over to the bed, he sat down and held me tightly. I blurted out
my accusations and waited for his defense. When I looked up
into his face, I saw tears brimming in his eyes. Instantly, I realized
what a foolish mistake I had made. After nine years of marriage,
how could I have doubted my husband's love for our little girl.

For the next half hour or so we talked about our differences in
grieving. As a woman, I needed time to be still, to think, and to
cry in order to process my emotions. As a man, my husband
needed to keep moving, keep going, keep plowing ahead with a
task or physical labor in order to work through the emotions that
swirled around in his head.

I rested in his arms and realized that together we had made it
through yet another step in our journey of grief.

Dear friend,
*My prayer is that as you and your husband sort out the thoughts, feelings,
and emotions surrounding the death of your baby, you would give one another the
freedom to grieve, each in his own way. May God's grace be upon you so that
this process draws you together instead of tearing you apart.*

The Rose Bush

by Joylynn Charity Miller

Once, a little rose bush,
With no blooms yet to bear,
Inched itself toward a picket fence,
And quietly rested there.

Then day by day it pulled its stems,
To the flaws in the fence's wall,
And slowly crept its way ...
Until it wasn't there at all.

On the other side it flourished,
On the other side, grew lush,
But the planter of the seedling,
Missed that beautiful rose bush.

So young and it had vanished,
So small and it was gone,
But on the other side of the fence,
It still, to life, held on!

And as the little babies here,
Have left without a trace,
They rest upon the heavenly shore,
And bloom in all God's grace!

Joylynn Miller, age 14, from Ukiah, California, penned this beautiful poem as a gift to her friend who had suffered the loss of her baby.

Roadway in the Wilderness

"I will even make a roadway in the wilderness."
Isaiah 43:19 (NASB)

The journey that follows the death of a loved one is a journey that I certainly did not sign up for. And to think that this journey of grief would not be over in a day or two made me want to crawl in a hole somewhere. With no itinerary, so to speak, I hated not knowing what emotions, situations, or circumstances I might face tomorrow or even six months from now. How my heart ached on this journey and it had only just begun. I can see why some have referred to it as a "wilderness experience." Feelings of isolation, emptiness and loneliness seemed all too familiar.

One Sunday, however, a single phrase in a praise song brought me the breath of hope that I needed. "Behold I will do something new among you.... I will even make a roadway in the wilderness...." God would make a way when there seemed to be no way. He would make a roadway through this barren, desolate wilderness. So what was I to do? Follow! Follow the roadway! Follow Him one step at a time through the twists and turns and over the hills and valleys of this wilderness until I reach the lushness of the promise land that He has prepared just for me.

Dear friend,

God has not abandoned you on this journey. Follow Him. One step at a time, one day at a time, through the wilderness. I promise a lush land awaits you, offering peace, hope, healing, and joy.

Healing Words

The tongue of the wise brings healing. Proverbs 12:18

"I am so sorry you lost your baby."
"My heart breaks for your loss of Molly."
"I just wanted you to know I am thinking about you."
It is so true that the tongue has the power to tear down or build up. While there were many careless words thrown my way after Molly died, there were also many words that brought healing. It feels so good to hear Molly's name spoken by someone other than myself or my husband. Healing also comes from phrases that acknowledge my loss as a *real* baby. One friend simply held me and said, "I just don't know what to say, but I hurt so much for you." Her words were like ointment on an open sore.

I am thankful God continues to bring people into my life who seek his wisdom and speak words that bring healing to my broken heart.

Dear friend,
This week my prayer is that you would feel God's healing power through the wise words of compassionate friends.

Christian Professionals

He who pursues righteousness and love finds life,
prosperity and honor Proverbs 21:21

I treasure the number of family members and friends who reached out in immeasurable ways during an incredibly difficult time in our lives. Beyond that intimate circle, I also feel blessed for the Christian professionals that God provided to minister to our family during our time of loss.

Our pastor and his wife came to the hospital as soon as they heard we were having a sonogram to determine if our baby had died. They were the first familiar faces we saw after the doctor confirmed that there were "no signs of a viable pregnancy." They hugged my husband and me and cried with us over the loss of our baby. Our pastor's words still echo in my mind. "No matter what, we will be here for you guys." And they were. The evening of Molly's birth, they came to the hospital again to hold our little girl. Two days later they guided us through the funeral service as we said goodbye to our tiny baby. We treasured them as our pastoral couple; but, even more so, we cherished them as friends.

My induced labor and delivery was a nightmare I thought I would not survive. But during those hours of anguish, God placed a compassionate Christian doctor by my bed. His words and actions revealed the work of God in his life. When our little girl was born, he blessed my heart by the way he gently held her and stroked her lifeless body. He knew our Molly was a precious child created in the image of God.

Six hours later we kissed our baby girl goodbye and laid her gently on the bed. The nurse had promised me they would not take her to the morgue, but would leave her on the bed until the undertaker came. Weeks later I found out that, when the undertaker came for Molly's body, he did not put her in a case or special box. Instead, he wrapped her snugly in a blanket and walked down the hall with her as if she were alive. The nurses all down the hall with her as if she were alive. The nurses all marveled at his incredible compassion. That very thought warms my heart every time I think of it. Over the next several days, he took care of all the details surrounding the funeral and burial of Molly and never gave us a bill. We found out later he and his wife choose to do this regularly as a pro-life testimony.

We praise God for these men, not only for their professional skills, but more importantly for their ministry to hurting people. With grateful hearts we say "Thank you!" to the following Christian professionals and pray that God will richly bless each of them and their professions.

Pastor Marlin & Lisa Nafziger of Bart Ministries, Christiana, PA
Dr. William Bradford of Lancaster ObGyn Associates, Lancaster, PA
Steve Shivery of Shivery Funeral Home, Christiana, PA

Dear friend,

Look around you and take note of the professional men and women that God has ordained to minister to you during this painful time. I pray you would be able to see these people as a gift from a God who cares about every detail of your difficult journey.

A Hole in My Heart

Incline Thine ear, O Lord, and answer me;
for I am afflicted and needy.... To thee
I cry all day long. Psalm 86:1, 3 (NASB)

There is a hole in my heart. A hole that some days feels so huge that it could actually engulf me. It's a hole that came from losing Molly. It seems like when she died she took a part of my heart with her. In actuality, though, I gave her that part of me. People around me know there's a hole in my heart. Sometimes I cry, sometimes I even chuckle to see how hard they try to fill it for me. Some of their attempts bless me, others irritate me. I know deep inside, though, they are doing it because they care about me.

I know I am going to be okay. I just need time. I need them to realize that pursuing a hobby, volunteering for a special project, taking a vacation or even having another child will not fill that hole. Nothing will. As time passes and I continue to grow in God's grace, my heart will grow as well. As I love and am loved, my heart will grow even more. And as my heart steadily grows, the hole will seem smaller and to some degree less painful. But the hole and the ache that accompanies it will never go away. Nor do I want it to. For it is in that hole, that a precious dream was lost and yet it is in that hole that a glorious new hope will take root and be found.

Dear friend,

You know the pain and the deep ache the hole in your heart brings. My prayer, however, is that God would show you the comfort and hope the hole can bring as well. Nothing on earth will ever fill that hole nor would you want it to. But cling to the promise of finding complete and total healing when you are ushered into heaven and reunited with the child that has for so long held that part of your heart.

The Hope of Heaven

*There will be no more death or mourning or crying
or pain, for the old order of things has
passed away.* Revelations 21:4

As I walked out the front door of the grocery store, I stopped to chat with an acquaintance I had met on a few occasions. After exchanging small talk, she smiled and asked excitedly, "So I guess you've had that little baby by now, haven't you?" Immediately, I felt my entire body tighten as her words registered in my brain.

The story of a pregnant woman ends happily with the birth of a healthy baby. It's an exciting event for everyone, even mere acquaintances. The problem was, my pregnancy didn't have a storybook ending. I shifted my bag of groceries and then quietly said, "Our baby died. She was stillborn." The woman's face immediately expressed sympathy for me. I knew she felt terrible for having asked the question and I felt terrible because she felt terrible! I hate when that happens!

As I walked home I thought about the encounter. "Oh Molly, I miss you!" my heart cried.

God's promise of spending eternity with Molly doesn't always seem real to me. That day, however, it did. As I focused on the brilliant blue sky, I felt a closeness with God. No, storybook endings don't always happen on the earth, but I know God in His awesomeness has written an ending to Molly's story that is truly "out of this world."

Dear friend,

When the promise of spending eternity with your baby seems so hard to believe, may you feel the power of God's presence so you can hang on to the hope of heaven.

Precious in His Sight

*Precious in the sight of the Lord is the death of
His godly ones.*   Psalm 116:15

For quite awhile after Molly died, I struggled with a question regarding her death. As a mother, the most painful thing to experience is the suffering of your child. The thought of my baby twisting and turning with pain before she died haunted me for weeks. How could I not have helped her? Worse yet, how could I as her mommy not even have known she was in pain.

Finally, I went to see the doctor who had delivered Molly. My voice trembled as I asked him the question I so desperately needed an answer to. "Did Molly suffer as she died?"

The doctor's face broke into a reassuring smile as he gently shook his head. "No, your baby did not suffer," he said. "For reasons no one in the medical field knows, her little heart just slowly stopped beating. There was no pain."

A weight was lifted from my heart as I heard those words. My little baby had just slowly and peacefully drifted away into the arms of Jesus. I thank God for the peace I have in knowing that she is truly with Abba Father, her Daddy God.

Dear friend,
God is watching over your little one. He treasures having your baby in heaven with Him! I pray this very thought would warm your heart and bring peace to your soul.

──── Mother's Day ────────────────

You knit me together in my mother's womb. Psalm 139:13

Mother's Day. A day of so many mixed emotions. A day that takes so much effort to hang on to the hope of heaven, lest I become swallowed in the emptiness of the present.

The emptiness of the day is so consuming I can't get away from it. It's everywhere. Women with newborns in their arms on TV, pictured in store flyers, strolling into church – everywhere. And whose arms are aching and empty? Mine. I should have been one of those women with an infant in my arms today. Somehow, though, I feel as if the reality of having a baby slipped right through my arms, almost like a vapor. One day she was a part of me and the next she was gone. I want to cuddle that little life but there is nothing, *absolutely nothing*, to cuddle.

There is a feeling of desperateness in my heart, but it is at this point that I realize I must focus on what I do have instead of what I don't have. And I *do* have something! I may not be strolling into church or appearing in a family picture with a newborn in my arms; but, nevertheless, I *do* have a child. I *am* a mother. The moment conception took place I was blessed with the gift of a child and the title of Mommy. Psalm 139 clearly states, "You knit me together in my *mother's* womb."

I am a mother of a little rose in heaven and nothing – absolutely nothing – will change that. And although I don't have my little rose in my arms today, I do have the comfort of knowing that a glorious day is coming when I will meet her and together as a family, we will spend eternity with Jesus.

Dear friend,
This is one of the hardest days to face with empty arms and an aching heart. It is normal to feel overwhelming grief and sorrow on Mother's Day. My prayer, though, is that you will not become swallowed in emptiness to the extent that you miss the hope of spending eternity with your child and the honor of being a mother today.

Listen To My Cry

The eyes of the Lord are toward the righteous,
and His ears are open to their cry. Psalm 34:15

I am constantly amazed at how many things are different in my life since Molly died. Some things are so obvious, they stare me right in the face. Like the fact that I don't feel my baby move when I lie down at night. Or that I don't wear maternity clothes anymore. Other things, however, are seemingly insignificant until they catch me off guard. When that happens my emotions seem to go into a free spin, totally out of my control. Last night I walked into the church fellowship hall for a special meeting. Because the meeting would not start for another few minutes, people were gathered in small groups just chatting together. I was about to join a small group of ladies when I saw another woman approach the group and playfully pat the swollen belly of my pregnant friend. A pang ripped through me and I turned and headed toward the restroom.

Such a small, seemingly insignificant thing, so why did it send my emotions reeling? To the casual onlooker, that pat was probably insignificant, but to me it was a powerful reminder that the life inside my womb was gone. That little pat a friend gives a pregnant woman is an acknowledgement of the life inside her. Friends don't pat my pregnant belly anymore because my baby is dead.

The world keeps on moving, but at times like these, when I stop and weep for my baby, I take comfort in knowing Jesus is watching over me and He has stopped to listen to my pain.

Dear friend,
I know it hurts to feel like the rest of the world has brushed right by you. But remember, Jesus hasn't. My prayer is for you to know that, when you need to mourn the loss of your baby, His ears and heart are always open to your cry.

Hold My Hand

I am the Lord your God. I am holding your right hand.
And I tell you, "Don't be afraid. I will help you."
Isaiah 41:13

The first few days after Molly's death I clung desperately to
my husband. He answered the phone, he answered the door,
and literally answered everyone's questions. He made arrange-
ments with the funeral director, our pastor, and the support com-
mittee members at church. I held his hand and he led me through
the events that surrounded the death of our little girl.

Before long, however, he had to go back to work and there
was no longer a hand to hold. Suddenly the world around me
seemed so very, very big. The phone calls, the visitors, the cards
and letters, the flowers, the tears, the emotions and the never
ending questions swirled around and around in my head, creating
even more fear and confusion in my already upside down world.
I needed someone to hold my hand. Someone whom I could
trust to gently lead me through the chaos of my everyday life,
through my pain and fear, and through my journey of over-
whelming grief.

Dear friend,
God promises in His Word that He is there to hold your hand through this
difficult journey. Don't be afraid. He will help you. My prayer is that you will
reach out to the hand that is reaching out to you.

The Plans of the Lord

The plans of the Lord stand firm forever. Psalm 33:11

How many times will I question every detail of my life over the past several months and how it may or may not have contributed to Molly's death?

"Maybe if I had called the midwife sooner ..."

"If only I had not worked so hard that morning ..."

"Why wasn't I more in tune to my body ... ?"

"Did that little bit of chocolate every afternoon cause problems ... ?"

Through the prayers and reassurance from my husband, faithful friends, and a compassionate doctor, I am learning that I am not to blame for Molly's death. Psalms tells me, "The plans of the Lord stand firm forever." I can know, as a conscientious mother, there was nothing I have done or could do to blow the plan God had for me or little Molly.

Dear friend,

Don't become obsessed with the "if only" thoughts that often occupy your mind. As a conscientious mother you loved and cared for your baby. You are not to blame for your baby's death. We don't always understand the big picture, and, as Christian mothers, we do not have the ability, even if we wanted, to mess up God's plan for our lives and the lives of our babies. I don't understand how or why God dictates or allows things to work out the way He does, but I know in my heart He loves us dearly and He alone is the Master Planner. I pray you would rest in that truth today.

Through the Eyes of a Child

*How great is the love the Father has lavished on us,
that we should be called children of God! And
that is what we are!* 1 John 3:1

A few days ago my little boy, Matthew, and I were working in the garden. While digging in the dirt Matthew found a small toy I had never seen before. "I wonder where that came from?" I asked out loud.

Matthew looked at the dirty toy in his hands and replied, "It's from Molly. She dropped it down from heaven just for me."

My heart melted as I realized the amazing perspective my four year old son had about his little sister. He truly believed she loved him and cared for him so much that she dropped a gift for him to find.

We have so much to learn from the minds of children, but we have even more to learn from their hearts.

Dear friend,

Our Heavenly Father tells us that we are His precious children. I pray God would help you and I both to become more childlike. Always trusting, always hoping, and always believing.

Am I Normal?

Oh Lord, you have searched me and you know me.
Psalm 139:1

I laugh, I cry, I smile, I frown. I hurt and I heal, I rejoice and I mourn. Up and down, back and forth. I go weeks and weeks feeling strong and then weep over a TV commercial advertising Kodak film. I feel like a conqueror, then two days later I feel like I have been conquered. I feel excitement as I celebrate the birth of a friend's baby, then I'm caught up in unexpected grief during a children's program at church. I'm all mixed up and yet I am all together.

"Am I normal?" I ask myself. But who knows what normal is anyway? I read material on grief, I listen to the counsel of friends, I search God's word and seek His guidance. And as a result, I have come to one conclusion ... I feel the way I feel, and that is okay.

Dear friend,
Please be assured there is no "normal" way to feel after the loss of a baby. If your days have turned into weeks of deep, dark depression you must seek professional help. But don't add additional weight to your heavy load by constantly wondering, "Am I normal?" Keep the lines of communication open between you and your husband and a few close friends. Then rest in the reassurance that you can indeed feel the way you feel.

A Visitor from Heaven

by Twila Paris

A visitor from heaven,
If only for awhile.
A gift of love to be returned.
We think of you and smile.

A visitor from heaven,
Accompanied by grace.
Reminding of a better love
And of a better place.

With aching hearts and empty arms,
We send you with a name.
It hurts so much to let you go,
But we're so glad you came.
We're so glad you came.

A visitor from heaven,
If only for a day.
We thank Him for the time He gave,
And now it's time to say,
We trust you to the Father's love,
And to His tender care.
Held in the everlasting arms,
And we're so glad you're there.
We're so glad you're there.

With breaking hearts and open hands,
We send you with a name.
It hurts so much to let you go,
But we're so glad you came.
We're so glad you came.

Reflections

The fifteen meditations contained in this next section have been written by contributing mothers. These mothers have either recently, or many years ago, experienced the loss of a child through miscarriage, stillbirth, or early infant death. Their meditations are recorded as "Reflections" since their writings occurred sometime after the loss of their child. As you will see, these mothers have reflected on the grief, hope, and healing they experienced while on their individual journey. While each woman's journey is unique, there is a certain comfort in knowing you are not alone in your feelings, emotions, and struggles that have followed the death of your baby. Along with that comfort, I pray that you would be strengthened and encouraged by the steadfast hand of God in the lives of these mothers.

Many thanks to the following women who so willingly shared a part of their journey so that other grieving mothers could find hope in their time of great sorrow.

Dawn E. Beitzel
Mother of Asa Jolan – miscarried at nine weeks.

Tamyra Horst
Mother of a precious baby – miscarried at twelve weeks.

Lena Mae Riehl
Mother of Josiah – early infant death, two weeks after birth.

Jennifer Saake
Mother of Noel Alexis – miscarried at four and a half weeks.

Linda Stockin
Mother of a stillborn son and two miscarried babies.

We Send You With a Name

by Dawn E. Beitzel

He who created you... He who formed you... fear not,
for I have redeemed you, I have summoned you
by name; you are mine. Isaiah 43:1

One night, when I was in the hospital, I closed my eyes to rest. I saw a picture of a little fellow that looked like my oldest son. I felt like that was *my* baby who was now with Jesus – a son. We named him Asa Jolan.

I love saying and hearing my son's name. Using his name in this verse from Mark 10:16 blesses my heart because it shows me just how precious my little boy is to Jesus.

*"And He took **Asa** in His arms, put His hands on him and blessed him."*

Dear friend,

Many mothers, fathers, and siblings have found a true blessing in naming their little baby no matter what stage of pregnancy or birth the loss occurred. Not every family feels comfortable doing this, but it seems there is a certain healing that takes place when you send your baby with a name you have chosen just for him or her. I pray you would feel a clear peace from God as you seek Him for His guidance in this decision.

The Shadow of Death

by Dawn E. Beitzel

Even though I walk through the valley of the shadow of death, I will fear no evil, for you are with me. Psalm 23:4

About a month after we lost our baby to a ruptured tubal pregnancy, we attended the SHARE support group memorial service provided by a local funeral home. Each member of our family carried a gift for little Asa. The sight of his little white casket made me begin to sob. I stood there, clutching his only belonging – a Pooh Bear receiving blanket given to me by a dear friend in celebration of my pregnancy. Tears flowed as I listened to the minister read the twenty-third Psalm.

That Psalm will be forever precious to me. It ministered to me so much. I still can't read it without crying. Asa was buried with his blanket, notes from his family, and Baby's Breath from each of his siblings. That day was a changing point for me. I felt like the heaviness was lifting. I believe, in some sense, the service helped bring closure to Asa's death.

Dear friend,

For many people the phrase from Psalm 23, "Even though I walk through the valley of the shadow of death ..." sounds so dark and hopeless. As Christians though, we need to seek the hope and comfort this psalm is meant to bring hurting hearts. Catch the ending phrase of verse four and hang on to the promise that God will not abandon you or your baby. Instead, He is with you, ready to carry you and comfort you during each step of this difficult journey.

Psalm 23

The Lord is my shepherd, I shall not want.
He makes me lie down in green pastures,
He leads me beside quiet water,
He restores my soul.
He guides me in the paths of righteousness
for His name's sake.
Even though I walk
through the valley of the shadow of death,
I will fear no evil, for you are with me;
your rod and your staff they comfort me.
You prepare a table before me
in the presence of my enemies.
You anoint my head with oil;
my cup overflows.
Surely goodness and love will follow me
all the days of my life,
and I will dwell in the house of the Lord forever.

He Restores My Soul

by Dawn E. Beitzel

He makes me lie down in green pastures, He leads me beside quiet waters, He restores my soul. Psalm 23:2

It is now five months since Asa's death. Throughout these past months, the tears would and still do come unexpectedly. But God is *restoring my soul* like the Psalm says. I still miss Asa tremendously, but God has brought me peace and joy again. I can laugh again. I can enjoy life again. God *is* good ... *all* the time.

Dear friend,

The word restore means "to bring back to original condition that which has been damaged." What an awesome promise from the Word of God. And who will restore your soul where it has been damaged? The Lord and only the Lord. It is not something we can do ourselves, nor can our families, pastors, or loved ones do it for us. My prayer is that you would surrender your broken heart and broken dreams to God so He can begin the delicate but powerful process of restoring your soul.

Where Are You, God?

by Tamyra Horst

*My tears have been my food day and night while they say
to me all day long, "Where is your God?"* Psalm 42:3

I had always dreamed of the day I would find out I was
pregnant. I tried to think of creative ways to tell my husband Tim
and our families. Maybe we wouldn't tell our families until I was
showing and they could guess. No, I knew I couldn't do that. I
knew the moment I heard those words, "You're pregnant," that I
would tell the whole world. I would tell strangers on the street.
Anyone who would listen.

I imagined what I would look like with my belly round with
the new life growing in me. Sometimes I would even stand in
front of the mirror and try to picture it. I thought nothing could
be more beautiful than a woman growing with the miracle of
God in her.

I longed to feel the movement of a child wiggling inside. I
pictured nights with Tim and I snuggled in bed talking to my
belly, feeling every movement. Sharing a joy that no else could
share with us. The specialness of knowing that our love had
planted a seed that would grow into our son. Or our daughter.

Now, lying in a hospital bed with an IV hooked in my arm,
silent tears filled my heart as my dream faded away. I had
wanted this child more than anything else!

Would my heart ever stop aching? Would the hurt and loss
ever go away? Did anyone understand? "Oh, God, how could
you let this happen? Why? It hurts so badly I can barely breathe.
Where are you, God?"

Dear friend,
God is with you. I pray you would allow Him to guide you into the loving
comfort of His presence. He knows your loss. How your arms ache! Allow
Him to help you in this moment when there is no understanding.

Endless Tears

by Tamyra Horst

You number my wanderings; put my tears into Your bottle; are they not in Your book? Psalm 56:8 (NASB)

The arms that ached to hold a baby now ached with the pain of loss. I wrapped them around myself, longing to be comforted, but found comfort nowhere. I packed the precious dreams of a child away, folding each one like a mother folds clothing her child has outgrown, holding each up for a moment, remembering – bittersweet memories – before packing each one away in a box, putting on the lid tightly and shoving it to the darkest corner of my mind. I needed to cry. I needed to grieve my loss. I had lost my child, my dreams for that child, my hopes. I wanted to share those dreams with someone. I needed someone to understand my loss. I longed for someone to hold me while I cried. Someone to cry with me.

Why had God taken the child for which I had ached so long? Didn't I take good enough care of myself? Was it my fault somehow? Should I have done something differently?

How could I explain how great my pain was? I had never felt this child move. I had never heard her heart beat. Yet I felt a part of me had died. I felt a pain so intense I couldn't explain it. Would I ever be able to laugh and dream again or would the silent tears in my heart that no one else could see ever stop?

Dear friend,

God knows your pain is indescribable. He understands the loneliness. The questions. His heart breaks for you. He sees every tear your heart sheds and saves them in a bottle. He writes your pain in His book. He weeps with you. May you feel His arms around you. May He give you courage to cry in His arms, to tell Him all the pain and loss and hurt. May you sense His presence and His tears, mingled with yours. May His love and tears, His understanding, give you courage and strength to make it today.

A Hope Renewed

by Tamyra Horst

I have loved you with an everlasting love: I have drawn you with lovingkindness. I will build you up again. Jeremiah 31:3

I had wondered if the day would ever come when I could smile again. I hadn't even hoped for laughter, just for a smile. A day when the tears would not threaten at any moment. I had been hurting so badly that being a friend, a wife, anything was hard to do. I had felt like I had so little to give. The loss of my baby and my dreams had been so intense. At times the loss had been all I could feel. But now I sat on the beach with the sun shining down on me, warming me like the hug of a friend. A soft breeze blew off the ocean and caressed my skin and tossed my hair. It felt so good. It felt alive. Like I was alive again. Like my heart was finally healing.

I watched as my husband played in the breaking waves just a little off shore. He was having such a good time. Acting like a kid again, he seemed so full of life. I wasn't ready to jump and play, but I knew I was healing. And as I watched Tim play, I wondered how long it had been since he had let down and had fun. Maybe he, too, had grieved in his own private way. Could it be that his own hurt and pain had been so intense that it had scared him and he couldn't share it with me knowing all that I was feeling? Maybe he, too, was healing. The hurt that had so enveloped me – and maybe him – had caused walls to grow around each of us. He seemed so far away at times. Maybe I had, too.

I wriggled my toes in the sand. It felt so good to be outside. To be away. Away from the office and the piles of work. From the demands and expectations of others. From the darkness that had settled around my heart. It felt like sunshine was finally beginning to break through. The sun, the sights, snuggling in

Tim's arms, all felt like gifts from God to be savored and enjoyed as if for the first time.

The love streamed down on me, persistently, like sunshine. God was loving me. He was healing my broken heart. And in a tiny corner, He was planting another dream. Another child. Another hope.

Dear friend,

Only our Father God knows what it will take to bring hope and healing into your life. Oh how great His love is for you! I pray you would feel His love in tangible ways as He brings healing for your pain. May His lovingkindness sweep over you and fill you with peace. I pray God would show you the way and the tools to healing. May you trust that His love is so great that He doesn't allow things to happen to hurt us, but that ultimately, He has something special for us in each moment of our lives whether it be filled with pain or filled with joy. May He bring you joy and new hope. And may he hug you with His love.

Wings Like an Eagle

by Lena Mae Riehl

They that wait upon the Lord shall renew their
strength; they shall mount up with wings
like eagles. Isaiah 40:31 (NASB)

Little Josiah, seeing you lie there with so many tubes and wires in your little body is more than I can bear. I am your mommy and yet I can't even take care of you. Do you think it is me who is poking you with all those needles and tubes? You look so perfect on the outside, but the doctors say there are serious problems on the inside. I cannot hold you, but I love to comb your hair, put Vaseline on your chapped lips, touch your soft skin, and kiss your tiny piggy-toes.

The doctors are doing all they can for you, Little Lovie. Daddy and I have been clinging to every ray of hope. There are so-o-o many unanswered questions. Why this? Why that? I asked the Lord for a vision where I could either see you in heaven with Him or home in my arms, or running with Sammy and Josh, but it was so clear to me when God said, "No, Lena, I want you to wait. Just wait on Me." Instantly the song from Isaiah came to my mind. "They that wait upon the Lord shall renew their strength; they shall mount up with wings like eagles." I drew such strength from singing that song over and over again. You probably have it memorized already!

Dear friend,
Oh, how difficult it is to wait on the Lord! During those difficult times in our lives, we have a tendency to seek strength from outside sources or totally give in to despair. I pray that you would wait on the Lord during this time of grief. He will renew your strength and give you wings of an eagle to soar in His presence.

Carried Home to Heaven

by Lena Mae Riehl

Wrapped in the warmth of our Lord Jesus, I shall wait to meet you in heaven. Psalms 16:9-11 (paraphrased)

Oh, Little Lovie, after suffering for two weeks on all those machines the time finally came for you to go into the arms of Jesus. After taking you off the ventilator, the doctor brought you in to us, wrapped snugly in a little blanket. Daddy held you in his arms while we sang songs proclaiming the promise of heaven. At one point you even started breathing on your own. What a beautiful sound! We had never heard you breathe during your two weeks of life so we felt like it was a gift from God. To hear each precious breath was so wonderful. As those delicate breaths softened and became more and more faint, I could just imagine an angel gently lifting you from Daddy's arms. Holding you tenderly, that angel carried you right into the arms of Jesus who was waiting to meet you.

Oh, Lovie, that vision in my mind brought such peace and joy to my heart. Life goes on Little Josiah, but daily I watch for His appearing and the time when I will be reunited with you, my precious son.

Dear friend,

Words could not express the glorious delight your baby is experiencing this very minute, because he or she lives with Jesus. It goes without saying that the death of your child brings tremendous pain, but I pray in time, it would also bring you tremendous joy as you think about your precious gem celebrating life with our Lord Jesus.

In My Father's House

by Lena Mae Riehl

In my Father's house are many rooms ... and if I go and prepare a place for you, I will come back and take you to be with me. John 14:2 & 3

Little Josiah, Mommy's Little Lovie, as I stand in the center of your nursery and look around at what was to have been your special place in our home, my heart is overwhelmed with precious memories of your little life. The long, white lace curtains frame the window as sunshine splashes on the wood floor, warming my heart as I am reminded of God's goodness. Your crib is clothed in white eyelet and although it never cradled your warm body, it reminds me of your innocence and purity as you are cradled in the arms of Jesus.

Little Josiah, there isn't a day that goes by that I don't think about you. And while I have no memories of you in this room, I know that there is a day coming when we will say "Goodbye," to this room, this house, and be ushered into our Father's house for all eternity! Oh, how my heart longs for that glorious day when we will say "Hello!" forever!

Dear friend,

No matter what stage of pregnancy or birth you lost your baby, there is a certain empty sadness because of the lack of memories in your home. There is really nothing that will make that sadness go away. At the same time, however, God can fill your heart and mind with thoughts of a new and glorious home that has welcomed your child and awaits your arrival. Ask Him to do that today!

But God, I Didn't Mean This!

by Jennifer Saake

In bitterness of soul Hannah wept much and prayed to the Lord. And she made a vow, saying, "O Lord Almighty, if you will only look upon your servant's misery and remember me, and not forget your servant but give her a son, then I will give him to the Lord for all the days of his life..." 1 Samuel 1:10-11

To say it had been an easy prayer to pray would be to greatly oversimplify the story. Such a prayer required a lot more faith than I could muster. What if God finally gave me this greatest desire of my heart, then demanded that I physically give my baby back to Him as He had asked of Hannah? I wrestled with the Lord for well over a year before I was willing to fully commit our future children to Him.

When I finally could echo Hannah's prayer, it really was easy because I thought I had worked through all the issues surrounding such a prayer. With great peace I told the Lord that I would give our blessing of children to Him "for all the days of their lives." I prayed with my whole heart, meaning every word. I figured I wasn't at great risk for having God ask me to take my child to a temple and let him be raised by a priest as Hannah had done, so what harm could come now by dedicating my children to Him?

Little did I know that within a year of making this promise, God would ask more of me than I was prepared to give. "A miscarriage? But Lord, it hurts too much! When I dedicated our children to You I just meant that we would raise them in a strong Christian home, teaching them to love and serve You. We have waited two long years for this Little One. How could you ask such a high price for faith?" I felt like a young child, afraid of water, finally jumping into a swimming pool expecting my Daddy to catch me. Instead, I found myself in over my head. I panicked and thrashed about, feeling that I would drown.

I had trusted God with my most vulnerable area and felt betrayed that He had not protected me from my greatest fear. At first I was too deep in my sorrow, too numb and hurt to listen for His answers. Only when my emotional reserves were gone, did I finally notice that the Arms I thought hadn't been there to catch me had actually been upholding me all along, even as I kicked and fought to keep from sinking on my own.

Dear friend,

It is during the times in our lives when we feel the weakest that God's power is made perfect. His grace is sufficient because it has been tailor-fitted for each of our specific hurts and struggles. I pray that you would rest in that grace and feel His power upholding you throughout your journey of grief, hope, and healing.

Rededication

by Jennifer Saake

*I am the woman who stood here beside you praying to the Lord.
I prayed for this child, and the Lord granted me what I asked
of Him. So now I give him to the Lord. For His whole life
he will be given over to the Lord.* 1 Samuel 1:26-28

I see now from Hannah's story that God never demanded
Samuel from Hannah. She gave up the joy of raising her child out
of her own free will, an act of love and adoration for the God
who had granted her request and placed this child within her
barren womb. I did not have the same choice in the matter of
raising my daughter. She slipped from my womb without my
consent. But now I do have a choice in my attitude. I can
continue trying to swim on my own, or I can rest in the
protection of my Life Guard who will not let me sink. With
Hannah, I choose to rededicate this child and my own heart to
the Lord, now more fully understanding the cost of this choice.

Dear friend,
*To give your child fully to the Lord is a decision that may seem so painful.
In the end, however, it is this very decision that opens the door to complete and
total healing. I pray that as you dedicate, or even rededicate, your baby to the
Lord you would feel His Spirit gently ministering to your spirit in a new and
beautiful way.*

Fear, Faith, and Peace

by Jennifer Saake

For God has not given us a spirit of fear, but of power and of love and of sound mind. 2 Timothy 1:7 (NKJV)

It took us two years to conceive Noel. Another four and a half years have passed since she slipped from my womb. As we have struggled to grow our family through several failed adoption attempts and continued fertility treatments, I've wrestled with many fears and doubts. "What if I can't ever get pregnant again? Do I even want to get pregnant again and risk this pain another time? If I do get pregnant, will I be able to enjoy the new baby or will the next pregnancy be bathed in fear? Will I forever be comparing my next child to the one I lost, feeling guilty that a new baby could take a special place in my heart that I longed to give to only this one?" I hate what infertility and miscarriage have stolen from me by scarring my heart.

Miraculously, the Lord has opened my womb a second time. Almost immediately, however, fears about my ability to carry this new child to term have threatened to destroy my joy and thankfulness. I do not know the Lord's plan nor what the future holds for us. Today, however, and every day until and even after our child is born, I must look to the Lord for His peace and strength in whatever circumstances He has for us.

Dear friend,

The loss of innocence that comes along with your baby's death is like adding insult to injury. It just doesn't seem fair! It is easy to slip into the bondage of slavery to your fears about the past, present and future. I pray that you would feel the peace of God throughout this walk of faith. Such faith can only be yours when you lean fully on Him rather than on your own understanding. May God help you to keep your eyes daily on His face.

A Memory ...

by Linda Stockin

Does not the potter have a right over the clay ...? Romans 9:21

In the first place, Lord, it wasn't quite according to *our* plans for me to be pregnant yet. But You allowed me to conceive, and I grew to love the baby in my womb for those five months. Then he was snatched away so traumatically! To go home with empty arms was an emptiness that can never be forgotten! And then before long, You let us miscarry two more babies. Lord, I didn't grieve much for the babies. I was angry and empty, and I was grieving for myself. I was so young, so headstrong. I thought I was so deserving! I wanted children and I was married! We would be such good parents! In my jealousy and self-pity I found it difficult to participate in the joy of other parents upon the birth of their children. Life did not seem fair to me and I was beginning to believe that our home might be without children. A sense of hopelessness and questioning had taken root in my heart. Lord, you were shaping a work in me that I didn't really want to be part of. Now, however, I can say thank you for not leaving me to myself. And thank you that You had an eye to mold me, to mold our family by Your own perfect design.

Dear friend,
I encourage you to hang on tightly to the truth and promises of God's Word. We cannot see God's final sculpturing of our lives, but what security we have in knowing the Great Potter knows just the work each piece of pottery will need to be made into a masterpiece. He is the potter, we are the clay! The potter takes special delight in you, for His pottery is the prized possession of His heart.

The Shepherd

by Linda Stockin

Like a shepherd He will tend His flock, in His arm He will gather the lambs and carry them in His bosom; He will gently lead the nursing ewes. Isaiah 40:11 (NASB)

My Lord, I love the picture of a shepherd tending his flock. Your eye is constantly on each one of Your sheep and each little lamb. You are gently leading us mama sheep along. You are there at our side, looking over our shoulders at our lambs. You know the heart of us mama sheep. You know how we love them, how we hope for them, how we ache for them, and how we fear for them. You can see what escapes a mother's eye and what lies in other pastures. You lead us along quiet streams that we may be refreshed. The rod and staff that You carry are a comfort, my Lord, because they correct us or pull us back from our wandering, selfish ways that lead to danger. We are Yours and You are our own Shepherd!

You have already gathered three of our little lambs (oh yes, they are Yours), and You have carried them away in Your bosom to a very safe, green pasture. I ached when You took them and I didn't understand. But you were teaching me to keep my eyes looking continually toward the Shepherd, to keep following. As the days have passed next to Your side, I have continued to learn to love You because You are my strong, kind Shepherd. And I have continued to grow stronger and trust Your wisdom instead of my own. Oh, how blessed I am to be a sheep under your care!

Dear friend,

My prayer for you is that the comfort of our dear Shepherd, Christ Jesus, may fill your heart with a refreshing peace. Let your mind be filled with the words of the Shepherd found in the Scripture. He will wrap you in His arms and help you to walk again. Hold on to His hand and follow!

The Lord – The Builder

by Linda Stockin

Unless the Lord builds the house, they labor in vain who build it.... Behold children are a gift from God. Psalm 127

Lord, twenty-five years have passed since You have taken our three little ones to be with You. We carried them, not in our arms, but only in the little house of the womb. You were beginning to build, not by the design that seemed right or fair to me at the time, but with Your own Master Plan You were building. You are each child's Owner and the Builder of each home. The days of each one of Your children are numbered, and the timing and arranging of homes is by *Your* wisdom for the accomplishment of *Your* purposes. Whether with or without children, whether rich or poor, whether with or without health, whatever circumstances – unless *You* build, we labor in vain!

Each home, Lord, is blessed with unique gifts from You. I am sorry I did not recognize Your gifts. I didn't even give thought to the fact that children were a *gift*, given by Your good pleasure, for Your own purposes. Thank you, my Lord, for those gifts you sent to us. You gave them for only a short time, but it was Your privilege to take back what You owned. They were Your instruments to begin to teach some very basic truths which their mama needed to learn.

Dear friend,
I encourage you to ask the Lord for patience as He is building your home. Can you ask for a willingness to accept the gifts He offers? Whatever the gift may be, even should it involve pain, know that He is accomplishing His purposes in the building of your life.

Chess Game Pawn

And we know that God causes all things to work together for good, for those that love the Lord. Romans 8:28 (NASB)

As the months passed since our baby's death, I, in my humanness, tried to figure out why the whole thing had to happen. I had lost two babies to miscarriages before and now I had lost Molly to a stillbirth. I remember several people telling me how the death of my baby actually helped them work through a particular loss in their own life. Another person said they felt they had been drawn closer to God through our loss. One person even explained how his marriage was stronger than ever because God had convicted him during this time of grief. For quite awhile I felt angry with God for seemingly using Molly's life as a pawn in a chess game. He put her on the front line and allowed her life to be snuffed out so that others "could grow closer to Him" or "heal from past hurts" or even "build a stronger marriage." Why did my baby's life have to be forfeited so that others could benefit? I confessed my struggle to our pastor who in turn shared some insights with me.

Molly died, not because Satan killed her and not because God chose to end her life. She died because we live in a sinful, fallen world where disease, sickness and death run rampant. But when Molly died, Satan saw an opportunity to wreak havoc in the lives of everybody around her. He would have loved to have seen our marriage, our relationships with others, and our relationship with God destroyed and he would work earnestly to that end. God did not take Molly's life. He chose, however, to use the death of our child to draw people closer to Him, heal past hurts, and even restore relationships.

Wow! What an amazing revelation! For the first time, I truly understood Romans 8:28. God allows tragedies to come into our lives, but He does not create them. He is a sovereign God and in

His sovereignty He causes them to work out for the good of those who have the courage to trust Him.

Dear friend,

I pray a hedge of protection around you and your family so that Satan's plans to harm you will fail miserably. May God take your loss and your pain and use it for good, for so He promises to do for those who love Him.

The Sanctity of Life

For our struggle is not against flesh and blood, but against
the authorities, against the powers of this dark world
and against the spiritual forces of evil in
the heavenly realms. Ephesians 6:12

Today is *Sanctity of Life Sunday*. A day set aside for the
nation to focus on the sanctity of life. Webster defines sanctity as
that which is holy or sacred. I think of our two miscarried babies
and our stillborn little girl and their short life in my womb. These
two words, *holy* and *sacred*, create a feeling of awe in my soul.

At the same time, a surge of anger charges through my veins as
I look at the statistics in my church bulletin. This year, 1,300,000
unborn children will lose their lives. As a mother, I had fought
desperately to preserve the lives of my three unborn children, and
here are 1,300,000 mothers that are *making the choice* to kill
their babies. The struggle inside my mind is so great as I try to
comprehend the horror of these statistics. Don't they know?
Don't they understand how sacred the little baby is that is grow-
ing inside their womb? Don't they understand the awesomeness
of this creation? Why was I denied my baby after it was given
and yet they purposely choose to throw theirs away like a piece
of trash? I just don't understand.

Dear friend,
   The spiritual forces of evil influence the choices many mothers make. They
don't understand because they don't know Jesus. I pray as you work through
the emotions surrounding this day you would be able to praise God for protecting
you in this spiritual war. Because you know Jesus, you are not deceived by the
powers of this dark world. Instead, you know in your heart and understand in
your mind the true sanctity of your baby's life.

Aborted ... And No One Cared

Your eyes have seen my unformed body.... How precious
to me are Your thoughts, O God! How vast is the
sum of them! Psalm 139:16-17

It is a picture that will be forever etched in my mind. I can see it as clearly today as I could some twenty years ago in Junior High School. It is the picture of a tiny dead baby lying in a heap inside a small plastic bucket. The baby had been aborted. This graphic photograph was on the inside of a pro-life pamphlet intended to force people to see and deal with the reality of abortion. It was a photograph more horrific than anything I had seen before.

Throughout the years, conversations and debates centering around abortion would always bring that picture to the very forefront of my mind followed by a sickening numbness that would settle in the pit of my stomach.

Now, years and years later, the picture is in my mind again. This time, though, the horror is replaced by overwhelming sorrow. When I delivered Molly she was stillborn at five months. But, oh, how we loved her! We tenderly wrapped her in a hand crocheted blanket the hospital had given to us and held her for nearly six hours. We took her footprints, we filled in her baby book, and collected little mementos from her birth. My husband and two children made her a tiny white casket with her initials inscribed on the top. We had a funeral service for her and grieved with family and friends. We made up a scrap book, wrote in a journal, and just before Christmas we placed a beautiful little headstone on her grave. We loved our baby more than words could say.

But the little baby in that bucket had nothing because no one cared. No loving arms to wrap around him, no memento to keep his memory alive. I feel such a deep, deep sorrow for that little baby. To be perfectly created, secretly knit together in his mother's womb, only to be killed and dumped in a bucket for the trash. Oh, how my heart hurts for him!

Dear friend,

Your grief in the loss of your child reveals the fact that you know the truth. The truth that life is precious and is meant to be treasured, cared for, and loved. Let us give praise to God that He has shown us that truth and that He holds the lives of precious babies in heaven, safe and sound, loved and cherished.

An Evaluation of the Heart

Test me, O Lord, and try me, examine my
heart and my mind. Psalm 26:2

Our pastor had said, in his morning message, that this verse was *dripping* with evaluation. It's true. Test, try, and examine both the heart and the mind. Total exposure with nothing hidden. When I prayed that prayer and asked God to evaluate my heart and mind, I was sickened by the areas of darkness He revealed. Somehow, over a period of time, a certain hardness had crept into my heart, and, in the process, an element of my compassion and tenderness had been pushed out. In particular, I reflected on my attitude toward women who had chosen to have abortions. I hated their sin, which is justifiable, but now I had begun to hate them as well.

At that point, I realized I had chosen to hang on to a portion of my grief after Molly's death, instead of handing it totally over to God. The result was an ugliness in my heart with which I had grown very comfortable. As I asked God to forgive me and cleanse my heart, I felt a glimpse of my compassion and mercy returning for those women. I want to get back to the place where I can hate the sin of abortion, but love the mothers as Christ does. I'm not there yet, but I'm closer to that desire than I was a short time ago.

So while Psalm 26:2 *drips* with evaluation, I found it has the power to cleanse and *drench* a person with freedom as well.

Dear friend,
Bearing the weight of grief and heartache does not justify the ugliness we may have allowed to creep into our hearts. Maybe you are struggling with your response to your husband and friends. Maybe it's your doctor, pastor, or even yourself. Whatever it may be, ask the Lord to evaluate the very core of who you are as a wife, friend, mother. If you allow Him, He will cleanse your heart and mind while drenching you with a new and glorious freedom.

⸺Hold Me Close⸺

*The eternal God is a dwelling place, and underneath
are the everlasting arms.* Deuteronomy 33:27

A very special friend of mine is pregnant and due only a week
and a half after my baby's due date. After miscarrying her first
baby, Kim and her husband tried for an entire year to become
pregnant. I was so happy when her pregnancy test came back
positive. Her dream of having a family was going to come true.

Yesterday she spoke with a sparkle in her eye and showed me
the spot on her swollen belly where she could feel her baby's
foot. At that moment I was as excited as Kim. The rest of the
day, however, my heart was heavy. I, too, wanted to feel the
bump of my baby's foot or elbow.

Sometimes late at night when everyone else is asleep, I lie
awake in bed trying to imagine my baby moving under the
weight of my hand. But no amount of imagining will bring her
back.

My womb is now silent and still. My heart aches because I
miss my little girl. My arms ache because they will be empty on
my baby's due date.

Dear friend,
*Late at night when your heart cries and your arms ache for the precious little
baby you have lost, I pray you would feel God's arms wrap around you. Know
He wants to hold you close and love you to sleep.*

Missing You

*For He is our God and we are the people of His
pasture, and the sheep of His hand.* Psalm 95:7 (NASB)

Dear Little Baby, how often I sit quietly, alone with my thoughts of you. There is just so much I wonder about. How would our lives have been different if you had not died? I miss your smile. A smile that I have never seen and yet, oh, how I miss it! I wish you could tell me, sweet baby, what color is your hair and your pretty little eyes? What about your personality? Are you a little ball of lightning or are you more quiet and shy?

Oh, how I long to have you with me! I look out at the evening sky and I see the awesomeness of God's power as He paints a spectacular picture for all to see. As I watch the sky change, I feel a closeness to you. Maybe because it draws me closer to God. Closer to the God that holds the answers to my wondering thoughts. And closer to the God that holds you.

Dear friend,

I know you miss your baby terribly. So many questions about your child roll around in your head with no one to provide the answers in this lifetime. Though you may not know the answers to some of your questions until you meet your baby in heaven, God still wants to give you the precious gift of peace. Peace in knowing your little lamb is resting in the hand of God and being cared for by the Shepherd Himself.

——— *A Hollow Due Date* ———

*The Spirit helps us in our weakness. We do not know
what we ought to pray for, but the Spirit himself intercedes
for us with groans that words cannot express.* Romans 8:26

As I looked out across the great expanse of the Chesapeake
Bay I couldn't help but feel small and alone. Today was my
scheduled due date. My belly should have been huge with the
anticipation of contractions starting any minute. Instead, I felt an
incredible emptiness inside, both physically and emotionally.

"I love you, Molly. I know so very little about you, but you
were and still are my little girl." My words were answered only
by the rhythmic lapping of the waves on the sand. My due date.
But both my womb and my arms were empty. The ache in my
heart was too much to bear. I wanted to pray but could not find
the words. I closed my eyes and sat in silence. No tears came but
my heart wept in silence.

Dear friend,
*Oh, how it hurts! The emptiness is so overwhelming. But during this time
I pray you would not struggle to find the right words to pray, because there
simply are none. Instead, be assured the Holy Spirit hears and understands
your every groan, your every cry, and your every tear.*

One Day at a Time

by Marijohn Wilkin
& Kris Kristofferson

I'm only human, I'm just a woman
Help me believe in what
I could be and all that I am
Show me the stairway I have to climb
Lord for my sake teach me
to take one day at a time

One day at a time sweet Jesus
That's all I'm asking from you
Just give me the strength to do everyday
What I have to do
Yesterday's gone sweet Jesus
And tomorrow may never be mine
Lord help me today show me the way
One day at a time

Do you remember
when you walked among men
Well Jesus you know
if you're looking below
It's worse now than then
Pushin' and shovin' crowdin' my mind
So for my sake teach me
to take one day at a time

One day at a time sweet Jesus
That's all I'm asking from you
Just give me the strength to do everyday
What I have to do
Yesterday's gone sweet Jesus
And tomorrow may never be mine
Lord help me today show me the way
One day at a time

——Creation's Gifts——

He will be like a tree firmly planted by streams of
water.... The Lord knows the way of the
righteous. Psalm 1:3,6

My husband and I recently spent part of an afternoon walking up and down the aisles of a landscape nursery looking for the perfect tree to plant in memory of our baby. I had some ideas as to what kind of tree I wanted, but nothing seemed to suit my heart. After walking around for quite some time and listening to the manager explain the pros and cons of different trees, I began to feel discouraged. "Maybe this whole thing was just a silly idea," I thought. "Why did I ever think I could find a tree to reflect the memory of my little girl?"

Just when I had resigned myself to the fact that the whole mission was a failure we walked around the corner of the building. There in front of me was the exact tree I had envisioned in my mind. Only six feet high, this ornamental Snow Fountain Weeping Cherry was full of long graceful branches. Each of the branches was in turn covered with beautiful white flower petals. The branches swayed and the flower petals fluttered in the gentle afternoon breeze. It looked like it was covered with lace. So graceful and so delicate. It truly reflected the memory of Molly.

That beautiful tree is now in our yard, appropriately planted right in front of our play area. Now when I watch my children playing in the sunshine, the memory of Molly is right there with them.

Dear friend,

A tree firmly rooted offers strength and stability. At the same time, it offers many smaller gifts that often go unnoticed. Gifts of cool shade, rustling leaves, even a graceful dance on a breezy evening. I pray that you would see God as that strong tree in your life, offering you strength and stability as well as memories, treasures, and reminders of your tiny baby.

Fearfully and Wonderfully Made

For you created my inmost being; you knit me together in my mother's womb. I praise you because I am fearfully and wonderfully made. Psalm 139:13

As I think about the day I gave birth to my little girl, my mind is filled with many good memories. I think about the six hours my husband and I spent holding our daughter, trying to memorize every one of her precious little features. Her tiny fingernails and little red lips were both shaped like our daughter Megan's.

Throughout the evening we asked close family and friends to come and hold our little girl, just as we would have had she been born at nine months. It was a special time as we watched them examine her feet, toes, fingers, and little tiny ears. We knew this would be the only time we would ever have to get to know our little Molly here on earth.

While holding my little girl snugly in her crocheted blanket, her little face made me smile. At five months old her thin little body and shiny red skin didn't qualify her for a "Gerber baby" contest, but she was my little Molly and to me she was beautiful.

Dear friend,

We had lost two babies to miscarriages five years before Molly was born. And, although we never had the privilege of seeing those babies, I do know, just like Molly, they too were fearfully and wonderfully made. I don't know how old your baby was when he or she died. No matter what the age, I pray that you would know your baby was and is a beautiful creation, fearfully and wonderfully fashioned by the Master's hand.

──── Troubling Thoughts ────

You understand my thoughts from afar. Psalm 139:2

Each week since Molly died I seem to struggle with a new troubling question. Sometimes after much thought and prayer I come to some kind of a conclusion about my question. Many times, however, my questions go unanswered.

Lately I've been wrestling with the question of whether or not Molly knows and loves me as her mommy. I know and love Molly as my daughter. My two other children share a bond with me as their mommy. But what about Molly? As my baby had grown in my womb for five months, she had heard my heart beat, my breathing, and my voice. Now those comforting sounds are gone. Does she miss them?

Molly lives in heaven now and I know she would never want to leave that wonderful place for earth, but does she long to meet her mommy one day? Or does she not even know I exist?

Some of my questions will never have answers, but somehow that doesn't stop me from wondering.

Dear friend,

God understands the thoughts and questions that eat away at your heart. You can trust Him with those thoughts. You can trust Him with those questions. Most of all, I have learned, you can trust Him with your child.

A Christmas Longing

Praise be to the Lord, to God our Savior,
who daily bears our burdens. Psalm 68:19

Excitement and laughter were all around me. It was Christmas! I watched wrapping paper fly off gifts and screeches of delight follow as a niece or nephew discovered their coveted gift. It truly was a time of celebration. I felt blessed to be a part of it all. For a short moment, though, I became lost in my own thoughts. This was to have been my baby's first Christmas. Along with the first Christmas the new grandchild always received her first Christmas ornament from Grandma. A twinge of sadness crept in as I thought about what would have been.

I focused my thoughts once again on the celebration around me. A little while later I was handed a small gift. I saw on the tag that it was from my mom and dad. Not giving the contents a whole lot of thought, I pulled back the tissue paper and the sight that met my eyes sent an instant shiver through my body. A gold crescent moon cradled a baby girl on a tiny pink pillow. Gold stars and beautiful delicate rose buds surrounded the sleeping infant. Printed neatly above the baby in a puffy cloud was the name *Molly Dawn.* I stared at the ornament and couldn't believe how perfectly it reflected my little girl. I looked up and saw my mom and my sister watching me with tears in their eyes. My baby had not been forgotten on her first Christmas.

Dear friend,

I know you are struggling with a certain sadness during your baby's first Christmas. Please remember, though, that God is a God who not only wants to bear our burdens, but He wants to give us special delights as well. My prayer is that you would find a tangible way to capture the spirit of Christmas and the memory of your baby together. It is amazing how God can and will use this keepsake to bring healing, not only this first Christmas, but also in the Christmases to follow.

The Gift of a Child

For unto you this day, in the city of David,
a Savior has been born; He is Christ
the Lord. Luke 2:11

When we get away from the hustle and bustle of the *man-made Christmas*, we can allow ourselves to see the *God-made Christmas*. How awesome to think that the very first gift of Christmas was a child. Yes, the heaviness of my baby not being in my arms for her first Christmas is incredible. Yet I realize in the midst of my sorrow, I must, I simply must, look at the first gift God gave to me. He gave me a child, His son, as a gift. If I look at this gift child and toss it away because of my pain, I could very easily be forever lost in my own grief.

However, if in the midst of my grief I accept this gift child from God, I will find hope, even joy, comparable to nothing else in this world.

Dear friend,
Grieve the loss of your baby and the emptiness of his or her first Christmas. But, I pray with all my heart you would not be so lost in your grief that you miss the first gift of Christmas. A baby. God's baby. Sent for you so you could find joy in the present and hope for the future.

The Death of a Dream

*The Lord is close to the brokenhearted and saves
those who are crushed in spirit.* Psalms 34:18

As I struggle to sort through my feelings since the death of my baby, I have begun to realize this journey will last until I am reunited with Molly in heaven. For me, this grief process involves more than dealing with my emotions surrounding her death. It is the continual process of working through the pain of broken dreams.

As a parent I dreamed about my baby since the time my pregnancy test came back with the little "+" sign. I dreamed about her physical appearance, her personality, her strengths and weaknesses, as well as her likes and dislikes. With the death of my baby came the death of all my dreams for her. I will never see Molly's first smile, her first tooth, or her first step. I will never be able to toss her in the air and listen to her giggle. I will never be able to walk her to Sunday School for the first time, put a band-aid on her skinned knee, or solve an argument between her and her brother. I will never watch as she steps off the school bus, participates in a school program, or turns red when a certain boy's name is mentioned. I will never pray with her over a job interview, watch her daddy walk her down the aisle, or see her blossom into womanhood.

Broken dreams. They started with her death and they seem to go on forever. Perhaps the hardest one of all is knowing I will never hug her and kiss her good night because I have already kissed her goodbye.

Dear friend,

Oh, how we miss our babies and the simple dreams they would have fulfilled simply by being in our lives. I pray you would feel the Lord's closeness right now. Broken dreams will break your heart, but God will not let them break your spirit. Cling to the awesome dream of spending eternity with your baby! I promise, this dream will come true.

A Child of the King

You have received the spirit of adoption by which we cry out, "Abba Father!" The Spirit Himself bears witness with our spirit that we are children of God. And if we are children, then we are heirs — heirs of God and joint heirs with Jesus. Romans 8:15-17

I have noticed how popular the topic of heaven becomes when somebody dies. Especially a child. Many people have the idea that heaven is this vapor filled fairy tale land where children and adults who have passed away, sprout wings and fly around on clouds playing harps. Thus the topic of angels often emerges with comments such as, "God must have needed another angel so he chose your little baby," or "Now you have an angel in heaven watching over you." While these comments are meant to bring encouragement, I can't help but wonder where some people get their teaching on heaven.

When my baby died she did not become an angel. As a child of God she went to heaven to live with her Abba Father, her Daddy God. Being adopted by God, she is now a joint heir with Jesus! Wow! Never mind the angels and clouds, she's a child of the King living in His kingdom!

Dear friend,

While angels play a crucial role in the world around us, I pray you would find comfort in knowing your child didn't become one of heaven's angels. Far better than that, your treasured baby is alive and well, living in a real place with a real King who has adopted her as His very own.

Happy Birthday, Sweet Baby

Yet this I call to mind and therefore I have hope:
Because of the Lord's great love we are not consumed, for
His compassions never fail. They are new every morning;
great is your faithfulness. Lamentations 3:21-23

The sky was gray and cloudy, lending itself to a blah feeling. Winter was gone, but the cheerfulness of spring had not yet arrived. Still, there was an air of excitement beginning to mount as the children and I tied the final knots on our birthday message balloons for Molly.

Earlier that day I had purchased a helium balloon for every member of our family. With the balloons bouncing along the ceiling of our living room, each of us worked to create the perfect message for Molly. Finally, we chose the note or picture that we liked the best and tied it to the string on our balloon.

To the person looking in from the outside, this whole activity may have seemed silly or even a waste of time. I knew these balloons would not float through heaven's gates into Molly's hands. In actuality, they would probably pop after we lost sight of them or drift away and land in a farmer's field sometime that evening. Still, there was a special feeling of inner healing as Megan, Matthew, and I worked together on this project. It generated memories and conversation about Molly's life in my womb and her life now in heaven. Although my children never saw Molly alive, there was no denying that they loved and cherished their baby sister. Their notes and crayon drawings clearly reflected that.

I explained to the children that the balloons would not really reach heaven, but that this was a tangible way for us to remember Molly and celebrate her birthday. My four year old, however, already had the solution figured out. "They don't need to go to heaven, Mommy; the angels will read the messages and tell Molly all about them."

I felt those familiar tears filling my eyes and replied, "You know what Matthew? I bet you're exactly right."

Standing in the backyard, we shouted a countdown and released our balloons. As we watched the balloons sail higher and higher above the rooftops and trees, Matthew and Megan simply could not contain themselves. Jumping up and down they waved and screamed with delight. "Happy birthday, Molly! We love you!"

When the tiny dots of color disappeared from our view, Matthew spotted the neighbor boy and shouted, "Shawn, guess what? We just wished my baby sister 'Happy birthday!' and guess where she lives? In heaven!"

Dear friend,

My prayer is that you would feel a certain spirit of celebration as you remember your baby's birthday. I know the pain is so strong but don't let that pain steal the joy, memories, and healing this day can bring.

But Joy Comes in the Morning

*Tears may last for a nighttime, but joy comes
in the morning.* Psalm 30:5

I remember so vividly the verse from Psalms being prayed over our family after Molly died. "Tears may last for a nighttime, but joy comes in the morning." This verse gives the assurance of the grief passing or lasting only for a time. With the heaviness of Molly's death lying on my heart, I honestly didn't see how the tears and grief would ever come too an end.

As I made my way, however, through the highs and lows of this journey, I slowly began changing course, without even realizing it. Over time, my journey of grief showed signs of detours that led to hope and healing.

Then one Sunday morning our pastor put a notice in our church mailbox, calling attention to an orientation meeting for parents who might be considering adoption. We had always wanted to adopt and we felt a certain curiosity about the orientation meeting. Several weeks later, we found ourselves seated with many other couples, listening to the presentation regarding the adoption of little girls from China. Halfway through the meeting, all heads turned toward the door to see a couple approaching the group. In the man's arms, his little Chinese daughter who was seven months old kicked and squealed as she looked at the crowd. Brian and I simultaneously squeezed each other's hand. At that moment we knew we were being called to adoption. With the death of Molly constantly on our hearts, we felt a confirmation that our little girl would be the *joy* that comes in the morning.

Even though we didn't know who she was, what she looked like, or even what her name would be, our family loved our little "joy" from the time we started the adoption process. For the next year and nine months we filled out paperwork, completed a home study, fingerprint check, and criminal clearance. We attended a workshop, read information updates, and completed more paperwork. We had endless fundraisers, wrote our life's story, got physicals, and completed still more paperwork. We waited and prayed through changes and delays from the Chinese government regarding our qualification for adopting. Our two precious children, Matthew and Megan, prayed tirelessly for their future baby sister.

To our delight, in the midst of the process, I became pregnant. I struggled almost daily with the fear of losing the precious baby in my womb. It took a conscious, deliberate decision to continually commit the life of our baby into the hands of Jesus. That commitment was tested to the extreme when I was admitted to the hospital with complications and had to be induced. When our infant son entered the world alive, well, and hungry we rejoiced! What an incredible blessing to deliver, hold, and *take home* a baby after the stillbirth of Molly. We named our son Micah Nathaniel which means "who is like the Lord" and "gift from God."

One month after Micah's birth, the agency called and gave us the news that we had a little girl from China! We felt the confirmation of God's hand on the entire process since we received this call on the same day we had said goodbye to Molly just two years before. When the FedEx man brought the package containing her picture and background information, the children and I nearly plowed him over. We ripped open the package and stared at the dear little face on the tiny photo. Two months later in a rundown office building in Changsha, China, Malia Joy Waltman was laid in her daddy's arms for the first time. A wide smile spread across her face the moment she heard her daddy's voice. The waiting and wondering were over. Our *Joy* had finally come.

Dear friend,

God watches over our families with the greatest of care, gently leading us through grief and on to hope and healing. He has a beautiful plan for all of us when we surrender ourselves, our emotions, our dreams, even our pain to Him. My dear friend, He loves you so much. Trust Him, lean on Him, and believe in Him. Because while tears may last for a nighttime, joy will come in the morning.

——— *Memory Ideas* ———

Many mothers struggle with the intense emotions of having *nothing* after their baby has died. There are very few, if any, memories, pictures, mementos, etc. Women often have a desire deep in their hearts to celebrate, pay tribute, or remember the life of their baby, no matter how brief their stay on earth.

The following is a list of ideas specifically for the purpose of keeping the memory of your baby alive. Several ideas are especially helpful if you have other children because it gives them a tangible, non-threatening way to remember their sibling. Create your own ideas or tailor fit any of these to meet your needs and the needs of the loved ones around you.

1. Write a letter to your baby. Share your heartache and sorrow as well as your dreams of heaven.

2. Make a memory box for your baby. Tuck any special mementoes, letters, gifts, or cards in the box. Add items to the box whenever you would like. (i.e., Christmas, birth date, Mother's Day, anniversary of his/her death) Look through the box alone or with others to rekindle the memories of your baby.

3. Plant a tree, bush, bulbs, or a cross in memory of your baby.

4. For your baby's birthday consider having a small birthday cake. Tie notes or pictures to helium balloons and then release them into the sky.

5. For any gift giving holiday, purchase a gift in memory of your child. Make it personal by choosing a gift according to the sex and age that your child would be, had he/she not have died. Wrap your gift and then bless a needy child in memory of your child.

6. When you are ready, consider organizing a small memorial garden at your church in memory of all the children who have died from miscarriage, stillbirth, or early infant death.

7. Choose an ornament in memory of your baby, possibly engraved or personalized with his/her name and birth date.

8. Hang a Christmas stocking for your baby and have family members tuck special notes or pictures inside.

9. Purchase or have someone make a rag doll in memory of your baby. Include the doll in family photos if you wish.

10. Stitch a nursery sampler for your baby.

11. Press a flower from your garden or flower shop reflecting the season your baby died. Tuck it in a keepsake box or make it into a bookmark for your Bible or another favorite book.

A Rose in Heaven
Ministry Resources

A Rose in Heaven $7.00
  A Journey of Hope and Healing for Women
  who Grieve the Loss of their Baby

A Rose in Heaven Audio Cassette $5.00
  A fifty minute live presentation by Dawn
  Waltman that will bring encouragement to
  grieving women and show others how to
  support a friend or loved one who has
  gone through the heartache of losing a baby.

Keepsake Memory Card $3.50
  Created by the author and her
  husband as a tangible memento for
  families who have lost a child.
  (5" x 7" frame)

Pastor's Packet $3.00
  A valuable resource to help clergy understand the pain and
  grief process associated with pregnancy loss and early infant
  death. Plenty of helpful counsel for relating to the parents as
  well as meaningful scripture verses, poems, songs and ideas for
  planning an individual or corporate memorial service.

For more information on the author's speaking topics, please call
or write for a brochure.

See next page for ordering information.

Order *A Rose in Heaven* (book only) online from:
   Christian Book Distributors
   www.christianbook.com

For all listed resources, call toll free
   1-877-302-Rose (7673)

or write:
   Heart Rhymes & Roses
   P.O. Box 83
   Intercourse, PA 17534
   www.Remember.TheRoses.com

Please add 15% for postage and handling (minimum $2.00).
For bulk orders or orders over $50.00, call for pricing.

VISA and Master Card accepted,

A Rose in Heaven Prayer Team

   A Rose in Heaven Ministries is blessed with a Prayer Team who faithfully prays for families who have recently lost a little one. If you would like prayer, or if you would like to find out more about joining our e-mail prayer team as a prayer warrior, please visit us online at www.Remember.TheRoses.com or e-mail us at Remember@TheRoses.com

Additional Resources

Hannah's Prayer Ministries
Web site: www.hannah.org

This is an excellent ministry that provides a wide variety of resources for women, men, pastors, or anyone who has been touched by the death of a child through miscarriage, stillbirth, or early infant death. Resources include newsletters, chat room, book lists, personal stories, listings of support groups across the United States, additional Christian support web sites, helpful links, and much more. Co-founder Jennifer Saake contributed three meditations to the "Reflections" section of this book.

M.I.S.S. (Mothers in Support and Sympathy)
Visit www.Misschildren.com for valuable information regarding all aspects of losing children. Founder and director Joanna Cacciatore lost her little girl and has now created a haven for grieving mothers to come and receive support, sympathy and encouragement, as well as updates on legislation, medical news, memorial ideas and conferences. An extensive online store provides a variety of resources that aid mothers and families in their time of grief.

Safe in the Arms of Jesus
Inspired by her infant daughter who died shortly after birth, Alice Craig created this beautiful pencil drawing to bring comfort and hope to others who have children in heaven. The drawing is available with one or two infants and comes in several sizes, note cards and Christmas ornaments. Contact Alice at (309) 925 2505 or visit her at www.aliceart.net.

Loving Memories by Meg Newell, Amy Zbinden, Alice Craig

Loving Memories is a keepsake journal to help grieving families in their journey following the loss of a miscarriage, stillbirth, or early infant death. Featuring Holy Scripture, poetry, and room for special photos and your thoughts and feelings, we think that perhaps the most consoling feature of this book is the remarkable stories, written by people who have experienced the loss of a baby. A valuable treasure to celebrate the life of a precious child. Order by calling (309) 266-1576.

I'll Hold You in Heaven by Pastor Jack Hayford

An excellent resource that answers many tough questions a mother often has after the loss of her child.

Available at Christian bookstores or order at www.amazon.com.

Grieving the Child I Never Knew by Kathe Wunneburg.